Cursive Writing!
An Introduction to Cursive Writing for Young ESL Students

By Donald, Robert, and Michael Kinney
©2011 by Kinney Brothers Publishing

Cursive Writing! Global Edition

A Kinney Brothers Publishing publication

Copyright 2011 by Kinney Brothers Publishing

ISBN 9781466241282

For information address:
Kinney Brothers Publishing
801 Range View Way
Knoxville, TN 37920-7600 USA
email: sales@kinneybrothers.com
URL: www.kinneybrothers.com

All rights reserved world-wide. No part of this publication may be reproduced, stored in a retrieval system, or transmitted, in any form or by any means, electronic, mechanical, photocopying, recording, or otherwise, without the prior written permission of Kinney Brothers Publishing.

This book is sold subject to the condition that it shall not, by way of trade or otherwise, be lent, resold, hired out, or otherwise circulated without the publisher's prior consent in any form of binding or cover other than that in which it is published and without a similar condition including this condition being imposed on the subsequent purchaser.

Under no circumstances may any part of this book be photocopied for resale.

For more publications by Kinney Brothers Publishing, visit our web site at www.kinneybrothers.com

An Introduction to Cursive Writing for Young ESL Students

Kinney Brothers Publishing

Dear Parents and Teachers,

Cursive Writing! exercises young ESL students in the primary skill of cursive handwriting. Simple, step-by-step lessons lead students from easy ABC practice to writing longer passages. While building students' dexerity and recognition skills, *Cursive Writing!* also introduces students to the pleasure of expressive writing.

Please don't hesitate to contact us at Kinney Brothers Publishing should you have any questions or suggestions. Also, you can visit our website at www.kinneybrothers.com where we offer additional support materials for downloading and use in class.

Best regards,

Donald, Robert, and Michael Kinney

Mon Tue Wed Thur Fri Sat Sun
Date / /

Let's write!

A

D 𝒟 𝒟

𝒟 𝒟 𝒟

E ℰ ℰ

ℰ ℰ ℰ

F ℱ ℱ

ℱ ℱ ℱ

Mon Tue Wed Thur Fri Sat Sun
Date / /

G

H

I

3

Mon Tue Wed Thur Fri Sat Sun
Date / /

J

K

L

Mon Tue Wed Thur Fri Sat Sun
Date / /

M *Mm*

m *mmm*

N *Nn*

n *nnn*

O *Oo*

o *ooo*

Mon Tue Wed Thur Fri Sat Sun
Date / /

P P P

P P P

Q 2 2

2 2 2

R R R

R R R

Mon Tue Wed Thur Fri Sat Sun
Date / /

S

T

U

Mon Tue Wed Thur Fri Sat Sun
Date / /

v

w

x

Mon Tue Wed Thur Fri Sat Sun

Date / /

Y

Z

Practice writing your initials! *MLK*

Let's review!

Date / /

A B C D E F G

H I J K L M

N O P Q R S T

U V W X Y Z

Mon Tue Wed Thur Fri Sat Sun

Date / /

Let's write!

a

b

c

11

Mon Tue Wed Thur Fri Sat Sun

Date / /

d

e

f

Mon Tue Wed Thur Fri Sat Sun

Date / /

g

h

i

Mon Tue Wed Thur Fri Sat Sun
Date / /

j j j

k k k

l l l

14

Mon Tue Wed Thur Fri Sat Sun
Date / /

m

n

o

p

q

r

16

Mon Tue Wed Thur Fri Sat Sun
Date / /

s *s s*

a *a a a*

t *t t*

t *t t t*

u *u u*

u *u u u*

17

v *v v*

v v v

w *w w*

w w w

x *x x*

x x x

Mon Tue Wed Thur Fri Sat Sun

Date / /

y

z

Practice writing your first name in cursive! *Mike*

Let's review!

a b c d e f g

h i j k l m

n o p q r s t

u v w x y z

Mon Tue Wed Thur Fri Sat Sun
Date / /

Write your full name in cursive! *Mike Hall*

Mon Tue Wed Thur Fri Sat Sun

Date / /

Mon Tue Wed Thur Fri Sat Sun
Date / /

Let's write these two-letter words!

an an
at at
be be
do do
go go
hi hi
if if
in in

23

| Mon Tue Wed Thur Fri Sat Sun |
| Date / / |

no   no

of   of

on   on

or   or

so   so

to   to

us   us

we   we

Mon Tue Wed Thur Fri Sat Sun
Date / /

Let's write these three-letter words!

cat

hat

fan

map

bed

pet

red

wet

Mon Tue Wed Thur Fri Sat Sun
Date / /

big

sit

hot

dog

top

bug

cut

sun

Mon Tue Wed Thur Fri Sat Sun
Date / /

Let's write these words in cursive!

mat

can

lap

van

red

wet

bed

net

pig

win

fin

mop

hop

pot

fun

run

Mon Tue Wed Thur Fri Sat Sun
Date / /

Let's write a self-introduction in cursive!

My name is

I am   years old.

Mon Tue Wed Thur Fri Sat Sun
Date / /

I live in

I like

Mon Tue Wed Thur Fri Sat Sun
Date   /   /

Let's write these sentences!

My name is Ted.

I am ten years old.

I live in Canada.

I like sports.

Emi is ten years old.

She lives in Japan.

She likes purple.

She has a pet.

Mon Tue Wed Thur Fri Sat Sun
Date / /

Let's write these sentences in cursive!

My name is Sue.

I am eight years old.

I live in England.

I can play piano.

Tim is six years old.

He lives in Spain.

He likes yellow.

He has a kite.

Mon Tue Wed Thur Fri Sat Sun

Date   /   /

My name is Jane.

I am ten years old.

I live in Australia.

I like green.

I don't like red.

I have a brown dog.

I can play sports.

I play volleyball.

Write the sentences on page 35 in cursive.

Mon Tue Wed Thur Fri Sat Sun

Date   /   /

Mon Tue Wed Thur Fri Sat Sun
Date   /   /

His name is Bill.

He is eleven years old.

He lives in Brazil.

He likes blue.

He doesn't like pink.

He doesn't have a pet.

He likes school.

He likes to study.

Write the sentences on page 37 in cursive.

Mon Tue Wed Thur Fri Sat Sun
Date / /

My name is Ann. I am nine years old. I live in Spain. I go to elementary school.

I like school. I like sports too! I like to play basketball.

I have a pet. He is a big brown dog. His name is Ben. He is a good dog.

Write your self-introduction in cursive.

Mon Tue Wed Thur Fri Sat Sun
Date   /   /

125 Main Street
Clinton, Iowa
52601 U.S.A.
June 12, 2011

Dear Sue,

    My name is Mike. I live in the U.S.A. I am ten years old. How old are you?

    I like to swim. I swim in a big pool. Do you like to swim too?

    I like to study math and science. What do you like to study?

                             Sincerely,
                               Mike Brown

Write a letter to a friend in cursive.

West Primary School
Beijing, China
March 5, 2011

Dear Mr. Green,

   Thank you for visiting our class. We enjoyed learning about Canada.
   Some day I want to visit Toronto. It is very beautiful.
   This is a picture of our class. We hope you will visit again.

                    Sincerely,
                    Pe Chin

Write a thank-you letter in cursive.

The Cursive Alphabet

A B C D E F G
H I J K L M
N O P Q R S T
U V W X Y Z

a b c d e f g
h i j k l m
n o p q r s t
u v w x y z

A Great Student!

_____
Institution

Upon recommendation of the English Instructor, this

Certificate of Completion

is awarded to

_____
Name

in recognition of the completion of *Cursive Writing!*

_____
Date

_____
Program Director

_____
English Instructor

CPSIA information can be obtained at www.ICGtesting.com
Printed in the USA
LVOW09s0752310314

379538LV00022B/4/P

9 781466 241282